The Good, The Bad And The Inbetween

Simrah Caratella

BookLeaf Publishing

India | USA | UK

The Good, The Bad And The Inbetween

© 2021 Simrah Caratella

Presentation by *BookLeaf Publishing*

Web: www.bookleafpub.com

E-mail: info@bookleafpub.com

ISBN: 9789357445849

First edition 2021

To my family and friends that have no idea I'm
about to publish this book

one look

The noise
In my head
It never stops

Thoughts of
Yesterday
Today
And what is
To come

But one look
At you

Silence

contrary

You see
They just don't go

Oil and water
Salt and sugar
You and me

We just don't go

self love

They say
I must find someone

Who would
Hang the stars
In the sky for me

But when I look
In the mirror

I smile
And say

I hang the stars
In the sky

For my damn self

hiraeth

That feeling
Of missing a place
I have yet to
Step foot into

A longing
For that place where

The sun
Shines a little brighter

Smiles
Are a little wider

And you and i
Love a little harder

two faced

Your face
Poets would
Write about

But your shadow
Demons
Would fear

I smiled
As I stirred my tea
And said

So, my love
Which me
Would you like
On this drizzly day?

koi no yokan

I don't love you
Not yet

But I feel myself
Falling
Slowly

It's inevitable

Your intense gaze,
I forget where I am.
I'm lost, yet found

The way you move,
Art.
I'm your aesthete

When you talk,
A holy sermon.
I'm your disciple

You're taking over me

Like an ocean
Takes over the shore

And I'm letting it happen

Slowly

It's inevitable

a woman's world

13

A woman
On the prowl
A silent force

An ocean wave
Beautiful
Strong

Oh, how she
Flourishes
In a
"Man's world"

Zeus
Is taken down

Aphrodite
Takes back
Her crown

born to die

15

If love is death
Then I was born
To die

I was born
To love you

coastline

The other day
I was walking
Along the beach

I saw the ocean
The waves
A constant motion
Ever changing
Like your affection

I saw a rock cliff
With jagged edges
Sharp
Piercing
Like your gaze

And I saw
A pebble
Black
Obsidian
Like your dark
Wretched soul

Of all the things
I saw that day
The black pebble
Was my favourite

audere est facere

Who are you to say
The mountains
Are too high for me?

Who are you to say
My flames
Aren't strong enough?

Watch me climb
Every mountain
And walk among
The clouds
You'll think me an angel

Watch me burn
Every cold heart and soul
Until they melt
In my presence
You'll think me the sun

I'll do it all
And more

Audere est facere

To do is to dare

ask eve

This game we play
Of give and take

Forwards and backwards
A twisted tango

It's reckless
Destructive

But I can't stop

You're an addiction
Of the worst
Yet best kind

I want more
And more

I'm not
The only one

Ask Eve
She understands

She knew the apple
Was poisoned

But she took
A bite anyway

illecebra

23

I know
I consume
Your every thought

I know
What it does
To you

The hunger
And restlessness
The sleepless
Nights

And I let
It happen

Because I
Like it

Because
I can

real magic

Magic isn't
Pigeons in hats
Or ribbons
In sleeves

Magic is
The way you
Carry yourself

Magic is
Smiling
In the face
Of adversity

Magic is
Following your dreams
Wherever they may
Take you

Magic is
Looking in the mirror
And loving

What you see

That's magic

damaged goods

And at the
End of the day
What do we really
Have left?

Except
The moon
Poetry
And our
Broken souls

phantasia

The other night
He loved me
In his mother tongue

And I loved him
In mine

astral love

I know you
From before
From millenia ago

I was
A moon flower
And you
Were the
North star

All I could do
Was admire you
From afar

Just as I do now

lucifer

You say
I put you
Through hell

Didn't you know?

I'm the devil
In disguise

Listen out
For the sound
Of my
Sharpened heels

You'll know
I'm on my way
To destroy
All that
You love

And then
Dance

In the
Wreckage

insanity

He's mine

I'll shout it
From the rooftops

I'll tear open
The sky

Collect the stars
In my hands
And shower them
Everywhere he walks

He's mine
He's mine

Yes
I'm insane

He made me
This way

And I'd let
Him do it
All over
Again

run

I dance
With the wind
Over hill tops
Far and wide

I run
With the wolves
Over mountains
Low and high

I run toward
A life
On the other side

divine horror

His touch
Sets my
Coal-like skin
On fire

His eyes
Otherworldly
I hear
The angel's choir

He is heaven
He is hell

My salvation
My damnation

a reminder

Breathe
You will be
Okay

Storms
Always pass
The night
Always ends
The sun
Will always rise

And you
Will rise
Again

Breathe
You will be
Okay